Living
LARGE

A Crocodile's Life

Sara Antill

PowerKiDS press.
New York

Published in 2012 by The Rosen Publishing Group, Inc.
29 East 21st Street, New York, NY 10010

First Edition

Editor: Jennifer Way
Book Design: Greg Tucker

Photo Credits: Cover, pp. 4 (top, bottom), 5, 6 (top), 7, 8, 10, 12, 13, 14 (top), 15, 16, 19, 20 (top), 21 Shutterstock.com; p. 6 (bottom) Jupiterimages/Photos.com/Thinkstock; p. 11 Andy Rouse/Getty Images; p. 14 (bottom) Bob Elsdale/Getty Images; pp. 17, 21 Jonathan S. Blair/National Geographic/Getty Images; p. 18 Anup Shah/Getty Images; p. 20 (bottom) © Morales/age fotostock; p. 22 O. Louis Mazzatenta/Getty Images.

Library of Congress Cataloging-in-Publication Data

Antill, Sara.
 A crocodile's life / by Sara Antill. — 1st ed.
    p. cm. — (Living large)
 Includes index.
 ISBN 978-1-4488-4976-5 (library binding) — ISBN 978-1-4488-5100-3 (pbk.) —
 ISBN 978-1-4488-5103-4 (6-pack)
 1. Crocodiles—Life cycles—Juvenile literature. I. Title.
 QL666.C925A67 2012
 597.98'2—dc22
                            2010047846

Manufactured in the United States of America

CPSIA Compliance Information: Batch #WS11PK: For Further Information contact Rosen Publishing, New York, New York at 1-800-237-9932

Contents

Meet the Crocodile

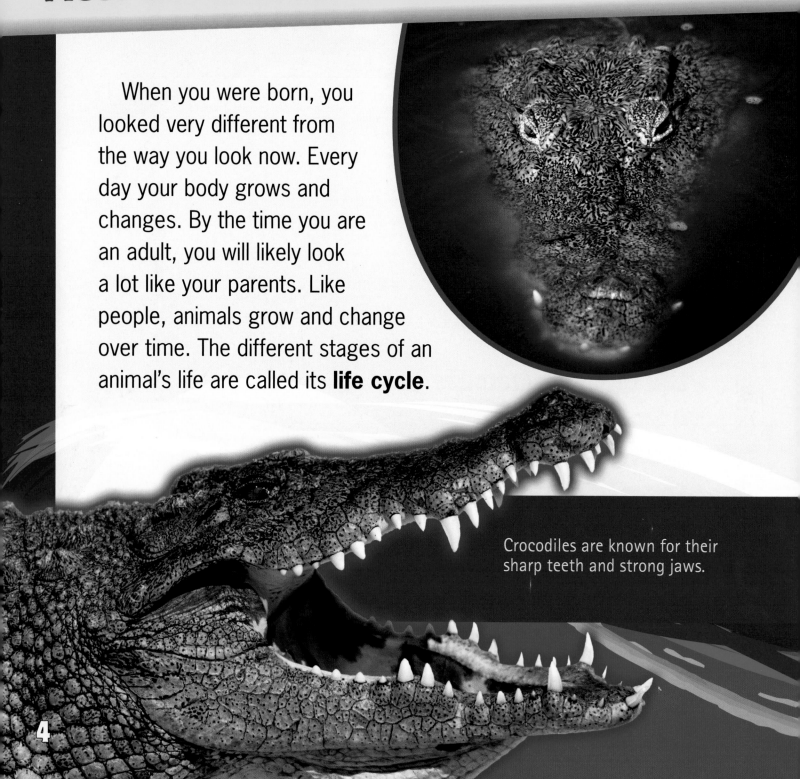

When you were born, you looked very different from the way you look now. Every day your body grows and changes. By the time you are an adult, you will likely look a lot like your parents. Like people, animals grow and change over time. The different stages of an animal's life are called its **life cycle**.

Crocodiles are known for their sharp teeth and strong jaws.

Left: Crocodiles sometimes rest in water to stay cool on hot days. *Right*: This Nile crocodile is in the early stages of its life cycle.

Crocodiles can live between 50 and 75 years. In that time, they grow from babies into adults, just as people do. Crocodiles lead lives that are very different from ours, though. Let's find out more about the life of a crocodile!

Big and Small Crocodiles

Crocodiles are **reptiles**. Reptiles are **cold-blooded** animals. This means they cannot make their own body heat. To warm themselves, crocodiles lie in the sun. To cool down, they may rest in the shade or swim in a cool river.

Above: This saltwater crocodile is warming itself by sitting in the sun. *Left:* The West African dwarf crocodile, shown here, is the world's smallest crocodile species.

There are 14 different **species** of crocodiles. The largest is the saltwater crocodile. An adult can grow to be more than 20 feet (6 m) long and weigh 1,000 pounds (454 kg). The smallest crocodile is the West African dwarf crocodile. An adult can be between 4 and 6 feet (1–2 m) long and weigh between 40 and 175 pounds (18–79 kg).

Warm, Wet Homes

Crocodiles can be found in many parts of the world. The Nile crocodile and the slender-snouted crocodile live in Africa. The American crocodile lives in North America and South America. There are other types of crocodiles that live in Australia, South America, and Southeast Asia, too.

Saltwater crocodiles are nicknamed salties. They are the largest crocodile species.

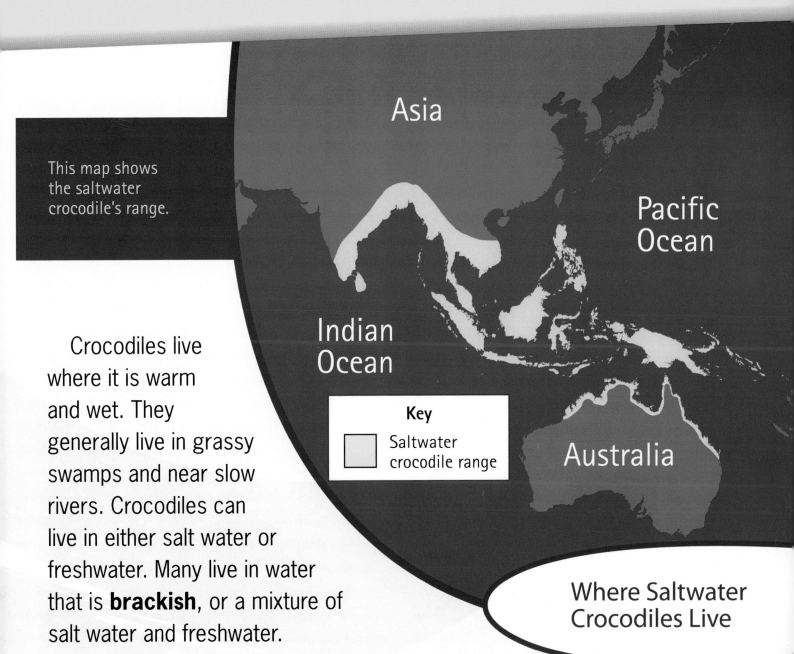

This map shows the saltwater crocodile's range.

Asia

Pacific Ocean

Indian Ocean

Key

Saltwater crocodile range

Australia

Crocodiles live where it is warm and wet. They generally live in grassy swamps and near slow rivers. Crocodiles can live in either salt water or freshwater. Many live in water that is **brackish**, or a mixture of salt water and freshwater.

Where Saltwater Crocodiles Live

Hungry Crocodiles

Crocodiles are **nocturnal**, which means they are active mostly at night. This is when they do most of their hunting. Luckily, they have very good eyesight, even in the dark! Crocodiles' eyes are on top of their heads. This helps them see their **prey** as they swim above the water's surface.

A crocodile's eyes are on the top of its head. Crocodiles can look for prey while staying mostly hidden in the water.

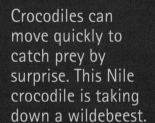

Crocodiles can move quickly to catch prey by surprise. This Nile crocodile is taking down a wildebeest.

Like many large animals, crocodiles are **carnivores**. They eat whatever they can catch in the water or near the water's edge. They eat mostly fish, frogs, and turtles. Sometimes they even eat monkeys and deer. Some crocodiles can eat half their body weight in one meal!

Sharp Senses

Crocodiles are great hunters. They have between 64 and 68 sharp, strong teeth. They do not use them to chew their food, though. Crocodiles either swallow their food whole or tear it up into large chunks to swallow.

The crocodile's sharp senses help make it an excellent hunter.

This is a close-up of a crocodile's nose and snout. Notice that you can see its teeth even when its mouth is closed!

All of a crocodile's senses are sharp. Their sharp senses help crocodiles hunt. Special parts in their noses give them a good sense of smell. This helps crocodiles know if other animals are close. A crocodile's sense of hearing is so strong that it can even hear its babies calling from inside their eggs before they **hatch**!

Life Cycle of a Crocodile

1 Baby crocodiles stay in their eggs for two to four months. When they are ready to hatch, they bark and grunt. This lets their mother know they need some help.
Baby crocodiles, called **hatchlings**, are about 1 foot (30 cm) long when they are born. They weigh around 2 ounces (57 g).

4 A female crocodile builds a nest for her eggs. Once the eggs are laid, she will protect them from **predators** until they hatch.
In some species of crocodiles, the males stay near the eggs with the females. Only a small number of hatchlings ever live to become adults.

2

A young crocodile spends the first two years of its life with its mother. During this time, it grows about 1 foot (30 cm) each year. Young crocodiles learn to hunt for their own food very early. They will eat mostly insects and small fish until they are large enough to catch something bigger!

3

When crocodiles are 10 to 15 years old, they are about full-size. Adult crocodiles are fast! A crocodile can swim up to 20 miles per hour (32 km/h) and run up to 11 miles per hour (18 km/h) on land.

A Small Start

Baby crocodiles are called hatchlings. This is because they hatch from eggs. Hatchlings are born between two and four months after their mother lays the eggs. When they are ready to leave the eggs, hatchlings use pieces of hard skin on their noses, called egg teeth, to break the shells.

A baby crocodile looks like a very small adult crocodile. The small bump on its snout is its egg tooth.

This mother crocodile (right) is tending her eggs while the father crocodile (left) guards them.

When hatchlings are born, they look just like their parents, only smaller! Although baby crocodiles start off small, they will keep growing for their whole lives!

Growing Up

When hatchlings are born, they crawl into their mother's mouth. It may look like she is swallowing them, but she is not. A mother crocodile carries her hatchlings from the nest to the water. She will care for them for about two years.

This Nile crocodile mother is moving her hatchling using her mouth.

This is a young crocodile. Young crocodiles are also called juveniles. This is the stage in its life cycle between hatchling and adult.

Young crocodiles grow about 1 foot (30 cm) each year. That means that by the time a crocodile is two years old, it will be about 3 feet (1 m) long. In those two years, its mother will teach it how to hunt and guard itself against predators.

Smart Parents

When crocodiles are between 10 and 15 years old, they are thought to be adults. This means that they are ready to **mate**. When a male crocodile wants to mate with a female, he splashes water and grunts. He may even blow water at her through his nose!

Above: Here is an adult female crocodile in Mexico. *Left*: This male crocodile is splashing around in the water to try to get a female's attention.

Crocodiles build nests by digging holes in the ground. The female then watches over the eggs until they hatch.

Many reptiles lay their eggs and then leave them unprotected. Crocodiles do not do that, though. A mother crocodile builds a nest for her eggs. After she lays the eggs, she sits with them until they hatch. This way, she can guard the eggs against predators that want to eat them.

Crocodiles and People

Crocodiles have been on Earth for over 200 million years. However, in the last 100 years, many types of crocodiles have become **endangered**. This is because people hunted crocodiles for their skin. People have also built too many homes and dams where crocodiles used to live.

This is a fossil of a crocodile. It is millions of years old!

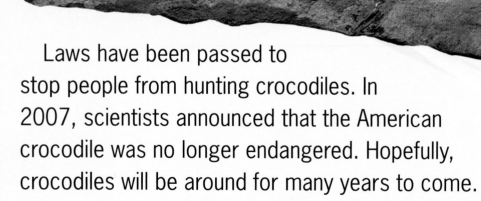

Laws have been passed to stop people from hunting crocodiles. In 2007, scientists announced that the American crocodile was no longer endangered. Hopefully, crocodiles will be around for many years to come.

Glossary

brackish (BRA-kish) Somewhat salty.

carnivores (KAHR-neh-vorz) Animals that eat other animals.

cold-blooded (KOHLD-bluh-did) Having body heat that changes with the heat around the body.

endangered (in-DAYN-jerd) In danger of no longer living.

hatch (HACH) To come out of an egg.

hatchlings (HACH-lingz) Baby animals that have just come out of their shells.

life cycle (LYF SY-kul) The different stages through which a living thing passes from birth to death.

mate (MAYT) To come together to make babies.

nocturnal (nok-TUR-nul) Active during the night.

predators (PREH-duh-terz) Animals that kill other animals for food.

prey (PRAY) An animal that is hunted by another animal for food.

reptiles (REP-tylz) Cold-blooded animals with thin, dry pieces of skin called scales.

species (SPEE-sheez) One kind of living thing. All people are one species.

Index

Web Sites

Due to the changing nature of Internet links, PowerKids Press has developed an online list of Web sites related to the subject of this book. This site is updated regularly. Please use this link to access the list:
www.powerkidslinks.com/livl/crocodile/